BALANCING HORMONE LEVELS IN MEN AND WOMEN

Hormone imbalance manifests itself in numerous common physical problems such as endometriosis, hypothyroidism, migraine headaches, uterine fibroids, osteoporosis, and urinary tract infections. Natural progesterone cream plays an important role in restoring balance to the body. One of the safest hormonal supplements, it is essential in regulating estrogen, testosterone, and cortisone, and aids in promoting and sustaining pregnancy. In both men and women, natural progesterone can raise depleted levels of DHEA and improve mood and libido.

ABOUT THE AUTHOR

C. Norman Shealy, M.D., Ph.D., is founder and director of
the Shealy Institute for Comprehensive Health Care in
Springfield, Missouri, the first multimodal pain rehabilita-
tion center of its kind. His many medical innovations include the introduction of the concept of transcutaneous
electrical nerve stimulation (TENS) and the first biofeedback
training program for chronic pain, which he introduced in
1972. Dr. Shealy organized and was the founding president
of the American Holistic Medical Association. He is the au-
thor of many books, including the widely acclaimed *The Cre-
ation of Health* (with Caroline Myss), *Miracles Do Happen,
Sacred Healing,* and the Good Health Guide, *DHEA: The
Youth and Health Hormone.*

Natural Progesterone Cream

Safe and Natural Hormone Replacement

C. Norman Shealy, M.D., Ph.D.

KEATS PUBLISHING

LOS ANGELES

NTC/Contemporary Publishing Group

Natural Progesterone Cream is intended solely for informational and educational purposes and not as medical advice. Please consult a medical or health professional if you have questions about your health.

NATURAL PROGESTERONE CREAM

Published by Keats
A division of NTC/Contemporary Publishing Group, Inc., 4255 West Touhy Avenue, Lincolnwood, Illinois 60646-1975, U.S.A.
Copyright © 1999 by C. Norman Shealy
Printed in the United States of America
International Standard Book Number: 0-87983-889-2
      02 03 04 RCP 18 17 16 15 14 13 12 11 10 9 8 7 6

Contents

INTRODUCTION AND OVERVIEW

Hormonal replacement therapy (HRT) has become one of the most controversial topics in American medicine. Conflicting studies about its safety and utility abound in the media. Some studies state that women who take hormonal replacement therapy have a decreased risk of osteoporosis, but an increased risk of breast, ovarian, or uterine cancer, while others show a decreased instance of breast or other hormonally related cancers among HRT users. Some studies show a decrease in heart disease risk; others do not.[1]

For many decades, the standard hormonal replacement therapy was Premarin®, a nonhuman conjugated estrogen from horses. Horse estrogen is many times more potent than human estrogen. Furthermore, it is chemically different from estrone, estradiol, and estriol, which are human estrogens. In addition, progestins are chemically altered so that they can be patented; however, much of their action is the *opposite* of progesterone; they *prevent* pregnancy instead of *promoting* it! Physicians have also begun prescribing artificial progestins, like Provera®, which has compounded the issue even more.

Progesterone is one of the two most important basic hormones in the body. The other, DHEA (dehydroepiandrosterone), is the body's most abundant hormone. More than any other known biochemical, DHEA has been correlated with health and longevity. Menopause occurs, to a large extent, when the ovaries stop ovulating, and the monthly fluctuations in natural progesterone come to a halt. Most women continue to produce some estrogen; however, minimal progesterone is produced after menopause. Progesterone is essential for men too; although men actually produce more progesterone throughout adulthood than postmenopausal women do, very little research has been done on the role natural progesterone plays in men's health.

In 1992, I demonstrated that supplemental natural progesterone will safely raise depleted levels of DHEA in both men and women.[2] The interrelationship between DHEA and progesterone was not previously known. One French professor of endocrinology informed me that there was no known way to convert progesterone to DHEA. Fortunately, hundreds of my patients did not know that! Although the chemical pathway is not known, the rise in DHEA after the application of natural progesterone is quite striking. This discovery was so important that I was awarded a patent on my research.

The health benefits of natural progesterone are legion, and include, among others, promoting pregnancy, increasing libido, and enhancing thyroid production. Most men and women can enhance their health after age fifty by using a biologically active progesterone cream on the skin. Unfortunately, many over-the-counter "wild yam creams" for sale in pharmacies and health food stores claim they contain natural progesterone when, in fact, only a few actually do. Obtaining the youth- and health-enhancing benefits of natural progesterone therapy depends on the quality of the product. This book will provide the essential information you will need to wisely select and use natural progesterone cream.

PROGESTERONE DEFINED

Progesterone, a major regulator of estrogen, testosterone, and cortisol, is the most versatile hormone in the human body. Even though it is manufactured in moderately large quantities by both men and women, it was originally thought to be a hormone that primarily assisted the growth of the fetus in utero (thus "pro-gest" for "promoting gestation").

As with virtually all hormones, progesterone is manufactured initially from cholesterol.[3] In fact, cholesterol is a major building block not only for hormones, but also for brain cells.

The major role of progesterone was firmly established in 1929 when it was shown that surgical removal of the corpus luteum, the small, yellowish bodies that produce progesterone and are found on the surface of the ovaries in pregnant women, led to a spontaneous abortion. By the late 1930s, it was known that the placenta produces 300–400 mg of progesterone a day during the last trimester of pregnancy. At that time, placentas were harvested after childbirth, frozen, and then later used for the extraction of progesterone. That was the only way to obtain it.

Fortunately, by the early 1950s, progesterone-like chemical compounds were found in thousands of plants, the most abundant precursor concentration being in the wild yam (*Dioscorea*), which produces diosgenin, a vegetable steroid. The simple addition of hydrochloric acid and warm water converts diosgenin to natural progesterone. The progesterone produced in this way is natural, and exactly the same, chemically, as human progesterone.[4] Logic might lead us to assume that the diosgenin in wild yam could be converted by the hydrochloric acid in the stomach to progesterone. Unfortunately, a majority of individuals over sixty years of

NATURAL PROGESTERONE CREAM / 9

age have an inadequate supply of stomach hydrochloric acid. There is no evidence that wild yam by itself can be converted in the body to progesterone.

Pharmaceutical manufacturers soon saw the value in turning diosgenin into natural progesterone. "Natural progesterone" is the term used for the human-made hormone, chemically indistinguishable from that produced in the body. It is not manufactured in a test tube from inorganic chemicals but is derived from a natural vegetable precursor. Because natural progesterone (which is chemically equivalent to that found in the human body) could not be patented, the pharmaceutical industry *changed* the chemical formula and began to make synthetic progestins (also called progestogens and gestagens) instead. Initially these artificial progestins were used primarily to prevent pregnancy; they are still found in many birth control pills today. However, unlike natural progesterone, synthetic progestins all have significant side effects, some very dangerous, such as blood clots, strokes, epilepsy, and so on.[5,6]

In other words, *natural progesterone promotes and sustains pregnancy; artificial, nonnatural progestins prevent pregnancy and may lead to abortion.* There are many other reasons to avoid progestins, but this simple difference clearly shows that natural progesterone is superior to any progestin.

Although progesterone has its most active quantitative production in the ovary and placenta, it is also manufactured in the adrenal gland—it is a major building block of cortisone synthesis as well as such hormones as estrogen and testosterone. Obviously, it is also manufactured in the male testes since progesterone is a precursor of testosterone. Interestingly, throughout life, men have much higher levels of progesterone and estrogen than do postmenopausal women. Progesterone production is much more variable in women than in men, as the hormone is made by the corpus luteum just after ovulation, and between ovulation and the next menstrual cycle, its production increases significantly.

Progesterone is the most essential hormone in initiating pregnancy because the survival of a fertilized egg and resulting conception depend upon it. The daily production of progesterone in a menstruating woman rises from 2 mg to 3 mg per day up to as much as 30 mg per day a week or so after ovulation. But if the egg does not become fertilized and implanted in the uterine wall, progesterone production falls off rapidly, back down to the 2 mg to 3 mg level. It is this sudden drop in progesterone levels which triggers menstruation.[7]

As with most hormones, progesterone is bound to a protein molecule in the blood, in this case, one known as cortisol-binding globulin (CBG). Progesterone is fat soluble since it is made out of cholesterol. (It is worth digressing for a moment to emphasize that, counter to the media anti-cholesterol hysteria, cholesterol is, in fact, essential for life. It is a major component of cell membranes and of all parts of the nervous system.) Progesterone-bound cholesterol circulates through the blood; at the cell wall it is dissociated from CBG to pass easily through the cell membrane, where, if there is a progesterone receptor, appropriate cells begin to use the progesterone for various life-sustaining processes. As progesterone is carried through the circulation into the liver, it is inactivated into and excreted through bile back into the bloodstream and out in urine. (This is one major reason for using transdermal progesterone.)

Progesterone in itself produces no secondary sex characteristics, and it causes neither feminization nor masculinization. Its most basic role appears to be as a precursor of cortisone, testosterone, and estrogen. However, progesterone does have many other direct or indirect roles, including assisting in water metabolism (especially excretion of water and sodium), increasing libido, enforcing thyroid function, assisting in the metabolism of fat for energy, helping cells use oxygen appropriately, stimulating bone growth, and many others which will be discussed later.[8,9]

In general, most hormones, with the exception of pregnenolone, a precursor for both progesterone and DHEA, are metabolically complete when produced. However, progesterone is a major fountainhead for producing virtually all of the other adrenal steroids including cortisone, androstenedione, testosterone, estrone, estradiol, and estriol.

In summary, natural progesterone is essential for producing a normal, homeostatic, or balanced supply of all the steroid hormones, mainly the families of cortisone, estrogen, and testosterone (see Figure 1). The important roles[10,11] of progesterone include:

- Balances endometrium (uterus)
- Essential for development of fetus
- Balances against excess estrogen
- Prevents osteoporosis
- Precursor for:
  DHEA
  Estrogens
  Testosterone
  Cortisone
  Aldosterone
- Prevents fibrocystic breasts
- Natural energizer/antidepressant
- Normalizes:
  Blood sugar
  Zinc and copper
  Cell oxygenation
- Helps burn fat and prevent obesity
- Optimizes libido
- Natural diuretic

Figure 1.
The Core Steroids

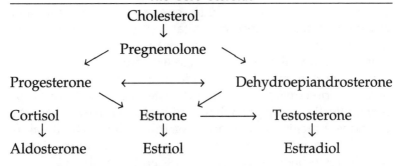

Cholesterol
↓
Pregnenolone

Progesterone ←————→ Dehydroepiandrosterone

Cortisol   Estrone ————→ Testosterone
↓   ↓   ↓
Aldosterone   Estriol   Estradiol

ARTIFICIAL PROGESTERONE: THE UNNATURAL PROGESTINS

Beyond making the pharmaceutical industry wealthy, progestins are excellent at preventing pregnancy and can be used that way effectively if taken orally. However, they have many side effects ranging from unpleasant to dangerous and I personally believe that there is no circumstance that warrants a woman deciding to use any of the progestins. All the progestins produce statistically significant increases in the incidence of breast and uterine cancer.

Progesterone is the only progestinol hormone made by the body. None of the synthetic progestins have the safety and natural benefits of progesterone itself. Provera, the most widely used of the progestins, carries a significant risk of abortion or congenital deformities in the fetus. There are at least seven artificial progestins, including medroxyprogesterone acetate, megestrol acetate, norgestrel, norethindrone acetate, norethynodrel, lynestrenol, and norethisterone, also known as norethindrone. The most striking aspect of these artificial chemicals is that they are never found in any living plant or animal.[12] Each of these molecules represents a metabolic endpoint: they cannot be converted into cortisol, testosterone, or estrogen. In my opinion, their only advantage is that they are patentable and make money for the pharmaceutical industry.

More important, Provera and other synthetic progestins have a long list of possible negative side effects: increased risk of birth defects, malignant breast tumors, loss of vision, thrombophlebitis, pulmonary emboli, cerebral thrombosis or stroke, liver dysfunction or disease, excessive vaginal bleeding, fluid retention, epilepsy, migraine, asthma, heart or kidney failure, depression, aggravation of diabetes, breast tenderness, spontaneous milk production, hives, rashes, swelling, acne, loss of hair, increased facial hair growth, increased or decreased weight, jaundice, fever, nausea, insomnia or excessive drowsiness, severe allergic reaction including shock, amenorrhea, high blood pressure, headache, dizziness, nervousness, fatigue, loss of libido, and impaired thyroid function.[13]

So why would anyone take Provera? It is widely prescribed to "balance" Premarin, the most prescribed estrogen, which I will discuss more fully later. However, one artificial chemical cannot balance another artificial one in the body.

THE NATURAL RHYTHM OF PROGESTERONE AND ESTROGEN IN WOMEN

During the first week to ten days after menstruation, the ovaries' dominant production is of estrogen, including the three different forms of estrogen: estrone, estradiol, and estriol. Although physicians usually mention estrogen when speaking with their patients, the estriol form is six to eight times as common in healthy women as either estrone or estradiol. Estrogen (especially the estrone and estradiol forms) assists the process by which the uterine lining builds up and thickens with the vaginal mucosa and mucous secretions, which make the vagina less irritated by sexual activity.

Progesterone regulates the pubertal changes in girls: the development of the vagina, the uterus, and the fallopian tubes. It also causes enlargement of the breasts, the buildup of subcutaneous fat that makes a feminine body different from the male, and the growth of body hair and increased pigmentation of the nipples.

Most of you know about the chemistry of menstruation, but for clarity, I will review it here. About twelve days after the beginning of a woman's menstrual cycle, estrogen levels (especially estradiol, which has a greater influence on the uterus than the other forms of estrogen) peaks and then falls as the follicle in the ovary matures to prepare for ovulation. After ovulation, the follicle becomes the corpus luteum and increases the production of progesterone. Progesterone levels, at 2 to 3 mg prior to the development of the corpus luteum, build to at least 20 mg per day at this point, and further enhance the development of the blood-filled lining of the uterus. An abrupt rise of body temperature at the time of ovulation is associated with the increase in progesterone levels. However, if conception does not occur approximately twelve days after ovulation, the ovum does not become embedded in the uterus and the progesterone level falls. The menstrual cycle then repeats itself. It is this interplay between estrogen and progesterone that explains menstruation.[14]

The anterior pituitary hormones control this process. Follicle stimulating hormone (FSH) drives the ovary to make estrogen and assists in maturation of the ovarian follicle. A day or two prior to ovulation, luteinizing hormone (LH) rises—it peaks just as ovulation occurs. The increased production of progesterone returns the pituitary's manufacturing of (LH) to its low baseline levels.[15]

Interestingly, the smooth functioning of this marvelous hormonal interplay is optimal in the late teenage years, but by the time women reach their thirties, the menstrual system often begins to malfunction. Perhaps this is due to cumulative stress or an unhealthy diet and lifestyle. By their mid-thirties, a majority of women will sometimes fail to ovulate at the middle of their cycles. Without ovulation, progesterone increase does not occur, leading to increasing problems with premenstrual syndrome (PMS) and an early predisposition toward osteoporosis. Stress can also induce an anovulatory cycle. Extreme dieting, even marathon jogging, can prevent ovulation or even delay or stop menstruation. Thus, the cumulative effects of stress in our modern, high-pressure society may predispose women to early, partial malfunction of the natural estrogen/progesterone rhythm.[16]

Despite the medical profession's preoccupation with estrogen replacement therapy after menopause, it is actually not estrogen deficiency but progesterone deficiency that leads to the menopause. Women's bodies never stop making estrogen unless the ovaries are removed. Some estrogen production occurs in the adrenals and some in fat cells. Unfortunately, at menopause, progesterone levels fall to nearly zero, well below the average adult male's level of progesterone throughout life.

Decreases in progesterone are associated with many of the health problems that affect women, including uterine fibroids, fibrocystic breasts, breast and uterine cancer, PMS, osteoporosis, depression, water retention, decreased libido, irregular and/or excessive menstrual bleeding, cravings for sweets, and excess deposition of fat, especially around the hips and thighs. It is estrogen dominance and progesterone deficiency that are responsible for these problems.[17]

THE ESTROGEN DANCE

As noted earlier, there is only one progesterone, but there are three compounds included in estrogen: estrone, estradiol, and estriol. All three estrogen molecules are present in all normal women. In pregnancy, however, estriol is the dominant estrogen. Even this relatively transient (nine months) increase in estriol production is helpful to women, as pregnancy, especially a first pregnancy before age thirty, is significantly protective against later development of breast cancer.

Among the many artificial estrogens, diethylstilbestrol is the most notorious, responsible for increased risk of uterine and breast cancer and male infertility in children whose mothers took this dangerous hormone. It was widely used forty years ago to regulate menstrual cycles and to prevent conception and premature labor before its side effects were known. It has also been used extensively to fatten beef cattle. Considering the long delay in medical recognition of the diethylstilbestrol risk, I wonder how long it will take physicians to acknowledge the Provera risk?

All other estrogens, estrone, estradiol, plant estrogens (xenoestrogens), and the petrochemical estrogens are potentially carcinogenic, particularly for the breast, uterus, ovaries, and probably the male's prostate.[18]

Furthermore, the pervasive use of estrogenic pesticides may also be a major contributor to the marked decrease in sperm production worldwide. The World Health Organization has lowered the benchmark for a normal sperm count from 100 million to 40 million per ejaculation. Note that a level below 20 million is considered infertile. Both the increasing infertility among college-aged men (35 percent) and the worldwide decreases in total sperm counts may well be the result of widespread pesticide contamination.

Even phenol, a widely used disinfectant, has estrogenic properties. The following are a few of the many hundreds of dangerous petrochemical estrogenic compounds: phenol, DDT, kepone, anthracene 3,9-D-dihydroxybenz, and many pesticides.[19,20]

The unintended hormonal aspect of these destructive chemicals disrupts biological processes in animals as well as in humans. Eggs that do not hatch, birds with bill deformities, pseudohermaphroditism, and unnatural sexual behavior in animals are only a few examples of the petrochemical estrogen plague. Animals of mixed gender (i.e., having both testes and ovaries) can be produced by use of estradiol or estrogenic DDT. Chemically castrated male seagulls and terns are produced by DDT or PCBs. In Apopka, Florida, in an estrogenic-polluted lake, 80 to 85 percent of alligator eggs failed to hatch and those that hatched had a tenfold increase in mortality in the first two weeks of life. Even surviving males had no testosterone and their phalluses were one-half to one-third normal size.

Many detergents, including everyday dishwashing products, are estrogenic pollutants. Such diverse species as fish, mink, otters, rats, gulls, terns, eagles, and humans all suffer from toxic estrogenic pollutants. Although this book focuses on progesterone, the artificial estrogenic environment of the late twentieth century may produce nature's greatest hormonal imbalances ever. The effect upon human beings of the inundation with environmental estrogens as supplements makes consideration of natural progesterone even more critical, perhaps even essential, for optimal health.[21,22]

Actually, estriol appears to be the one safe estrogen replacement. There is considerable evidence that estriol actually prevents excess proliferation or growth of breast and uterine tissue. In animal studies, estriol is almost as effective in preventing breast cancer as is tamoxifen, a drug often used to help prevent recurrent breast cancer in women. And there are virtually no significant side effects of estriol supplementation.

Premarin, however, which is the most commonly prescribed postmenopausal hormone, contains no estriol. The negative results of estrogen excess may occur from estrone, estradiol, or Premarin. Premarin is horse estrogen and is at least eight times as potent as human estrogen. Moreover, women have no enzymes to metabolize equilin (horse estrogen). Premarin also has 75 percent estrone, which is never naturally dominant in humans.

Premarin has been the leading prescription estrogen replacement despite the fact that its benefits for osteoporosis largely disappear after the first five years. Furthermore, there is a striking increase in uterine cancer in women on Premarin, unless it is balanced with natural progesterone.

An excess of estrogen in women has the potential side effects of increasing PMS, depression, obesity, dysmenorrhea, tender breasts, fibrocystic disease, fibroids of the uterus, swelling or water retention, low libido, breast and uterine cancer, pituitary prolactinemia (which causes mild secretion of breast milk), gallstones (cholelithiasis), liver dysfunction, and relative hypothyroidism with possible increase in thyroid stimulating hormone (TSH), but normal T3 and T4 in serum.[23]

THE ROLE OF PROGESTERONE IN MEN

As indicated earlier, progesterone levels are much higher in adult men throughout life than they are in postmenopausal women. Despite this, relatively little research has been done on progesterone in men. Interestingly, there are progesterone-binding sites on the surface of sperm and there are defects in progesterone receptors in the sperm of infertile males. The excess of estrogen in our environment may influence these defects. Progesterone appears to be important as one of the regulatory mechanisms in the production of sperm. It is also critical to recognize that progesterone regulates calcium uptake in human sperm, but this is not surprising considering that it has a very important role in calcium metabolism in bone.[23,24,25]

As mentioned earlier, in 1992 I suspected that males at age fifty who enter a period of change in hormonal production, sometimes called andropause, might have a decrease in natural progesterone production just as women do at that age. We then proceeded to have adult men apply natural progesterone cream to the scrotal skin and found remarkable improvements in mood, libido, and DHEA.

Although it had not been previously thought that progesterone could be converted into DHEA, we have recently been able to demonstrate that at least two-thirds of individuals, both male and female, will have significant increases in DHEA levels ranging from 30 to 100 percent over their baseline when they apply natural progesterone cream to the skin at the rate of ¼ teaspoon twice a day. This is equivalent to approximately 100 to 120 mg of natural progesterone. Perhaps even more important is the finding that exogenous progesterone does not interfere with the body's production of progesterone. Supplemental progesterone is simply additive. Thus, *natural progesterone is the only known replacement hormone which does not suppress or turn off the body's own production of that hormone.*

HORMONALLY DEPENDENT CANCER IN MEN

In men, prostate cancer is strongly correlated with testosterone, the hormone which distinguishes men from women. Testosterone is responsible for beards, male baldness, and secondary male characteristics. Baldness, benign prostatic hypertrophy (BPH), and prostatic cancer appear to be correlated, not with total testosterone, but with dihydrotestosterone. The conversion of testosterone to dihydrotestosterone is best prevented by saw palmetto, a natural herbal extract. Thus, as a safety feature, I recommend that all men start taking saw palmetto, at 160 mg twice a day, no later than age fifty. Men who bald early or develop BPH symptoms before age fifty should also take saw palmetto. Those with BPH should take 160 mg four times a day.

Since I recommend progesterone cream for men with suboptimal levels of DHEA, it is important to understand that DHEA may increase testosterone production. Thus, progesterone may increase testosterone. That is why, as stated above, all men who use progesterone should also take saw palmetto. We have now demonstrated that the level of DHEA is increased 30 to over 100 percent with the application of natural progesterone cream, with no adverse effects. In fact, I now have a patent on the use of progesterone to increase DHEA.

The best news about progesterone for men is that Dr.

John Lee reports in his *Medical Letter*, January 1999, that progesterone *blocks* conversion of testosterone to dihydrotestosterone. Thus, progesterone helps *prevent* prostate enlargement.

COMMON PHYSICAL PROBLEMS RELATED TO HORMONE IMBALANCE: HOW NATURAL PROGESTERONE CREAM CAN HELP

CERVICAL DYSPLASIA

Even more common than cancer of the cervix, cervical dysplasia or erosion, diagnosed by pelvic exam and Pap smear, appears to be related to hormonal imbalance. Progesterone or estriol cream applied intravaginally daily between menses may restore normal cervix epithelium. Folic acid (5 mg), B_6 (50–100 mg), and magnesium taurate (375 mg) should also be taken each day. This natural approach would greatly reduce a woman's need for cervical biopsies and hysterectomy.

Irritation, inflammation, and dysplasia or "precancer" of the cervix are so common that women are advised to have yearly pap smears which can pick up a precancerous condition before it changes into cancer. Those precancerous changes are probably related to progesterone deficiency to a significant degree, but also may be related to vitamin B_6, folic acid, and magnesium deficiencies. Three to 5 mg of folic acid, 50–100 mg of vitamin B_6, 400 IU of vitamin E a day, and 300–500 mg of magnesium per day, plus natural progesterone cream, are mutually helpful. In addition, fifteen minutes of relaxation twice a day, adequate physical exercise, avoiding smoking, and minimizing intake of dietary sugar, animal fats, and artificially hydrogenated fats are also recommended.[26,27,28]

ENDOMETRIAL CARCINOMA

The only known cause of uterine cancer is excess estrogen due to inadequate progesterone or to estrogen replacement without the concomitant use of natural progesterone. It is not enough for a woman to take Provera and the progestins to try to prevent uterine cancer. Supplementation is often inadequate and, moreover, significantly increases the incidence of uterine and breast cancer. However, Dr. John Lee reports that natural progesterone will not only prevent cancers of the breast or uterus, but may also prevent recurrence or metastases of the cancers.[29] He believes that having an adequate level of progesterone to balance excess estrogen prevents 90 percent of breast cancers.

ENDOMETRIOSIS

Endometriosis is an extremely painful disorder that occurs when some part of the lining of the uterus or the endometrium migrates along the fallopian tubes out into the pelvis, onto the ovaries, or even onto the bladder or colon. Since these cells are natural parts of the uterine lining, they behave just as the uterus does, swelling with blood during the month and bleeding at the time of the menstrual period. This causes considerable pain, especially during menstruation, and since they don't exit the uterus, drops of blood become embedded and lead to increasing scarring and inflammation.

Medical treatment using synthetic estrogen or progestins for this condition has been unsuccessful. In fact, estrogen, Provera, and other artificial progestins actually aggravate endometriosis. Interestingly, pregnancy is a remarkably good treatment for endometriosis; it's not understood exactly what happens to the endometrial tissue that has migrated to the pelvis prior to the pregnancy, but it disappears.

Treatment of endometriosis with natural progesterone, as one might expect, gives a much more satisfactory outcome than do synthetics.

Progesterone inhibits FSH and LH, as indicated earlier, so it is recommended that women use adequate natural progesterone from day 10 to 12 until day 26 to 28 of their cycles with a dose high enough to relieve pelvic pains. Dr. John Lee has reported that in approximately twelve years of applying this treatment, none of his patients with mild to moderate endometriosis has had to resort to surgery to correct the condition.

FIBROCYSTIC BREAST DISEASE

A majority of women have a small to moderate amount of fibrocystic breast disease that may or may not be associated with breast tenderness in the premenstrual or menstrual time. This problem has been found to be strongly correlated with the intake of caffeine, especially from coffee and soft drinks. The major treatment of fibrocystic breasts includes avoidance of caffeine and adequate use of natural progesterone during the two weeks before the onset of the menstrual cycle. It takes two to four months for fibrocystic lumps to disappear.

HYPOTHYROIDISM

Unopposed estrogen dominance can interfere with thyroid hormone activity and is a common cause of thyroid dysfunction. Commonly observed symptoms of hypothyroidism (underactive thyroid) include fatigue, constipation, muscle weakness, memory loss, infertility, swelling of hands, feet, and eyelids, dry skin, intolerance to cold and heat, indigestion, menstrual disorders, sleep disorders, loss of hair, emotional instability, premenstrual syndrome, and weight gain.

Estrogen and thyroid are two hormones that have many opposing actions, probably at the thyroid hormone–receptor level. Unopposed estrogen will prevent the thyroid from performing its normal activities and can lead to relative hypothyroidism despite normal blood levels of thyroid hormone. Progesterone, being a normal counterbalance to estrogen, inhibits many of estrogen's undesirable effects, including its interference with thyroid hormone activity. I strongly suspect that a majority of women with mild hypothyroidism would be better treated with progesterone than with thyroid. When there is estrogen dominance, there is also a decrease of libido with mood swings and irritability, depression, and headaches, all symptoms of hypothyroidism. Natural progesterone is the source of libido or sex drive in women and markedly increases libido in men.

Another contributor to hypothyroidism is iodine deficiency. Over eighty-five years ago, we thought we had solved the problem of widespread iodine deficiency by adding iodine to salt. Unfortunately, for the past fifty years physicians have recommended minimized salt intake. During this same time the entire world has suffered a marked increase in nuclear radiation; ironically, it is the thyroid gland that is the most sensitive organ to radiation damage. Finally, we have been advised to increase our intake of cabbage, broccoli, and cauliflower (the *brassica* family) for their protective effects upon the colon. But all these foods block thyroid use of iodine to make thyroid hormone. Ninety percent of individuals we see have low body temperatures, a prime feature of hypothyroidism. Iodine replacement restores normal body temperature. Thus, individuals with low body temperatures may suffer even more because of either estrogen dominance or progesterone deficiency or both.

For those with low body temperatures, we recommend iodine supplementation of 1.0 mg per day for six weeks. If body temperature comes up to normal (97.6°F in A.M. and 98.6°F in P.M., taken orally), then continue with just 300 to 400 micrograms per day.

MENOPAUSE

All women eventually go through menopause. Indeed, the internal hormonal thermostat, as indicated earlier, often seems to misfire even in the thirties. Virtually all women complete menopause by age fifty-five, although a rare woman continues the menstrual cycling as late as age sixty. A number of symptoms may appear as menopause approaches: irregular periods, excess or deficient menstruation, vaginal dryness/painful intercourse, decreased libido, hot flashes, thinning skin, reduced immunity/delayed healing, memory problems, forgetfulness, insomnia, depression, increased risk of osteoporosis, and heart disease.

Very rarely postmenopausal women will have spotting with the introduction of 3 percent natural progesterone cream. Here again, various dosages need to be tried to obtain the best result. Start with ¼ teaspoon twice a day and increase to four times per day if needed. One most interesting result of progesterone taken postmenopausally is the loss of facial hair and the restoration of thinned scalp hair, two fairly common events in aging women.

If menopausal symptoms persist after four to six weeks, add an herbal phytoestrogen such as Herbal-F®, up to six per day. Add estriol (2.5 to 5 mg) only if the phytoestrogens do not give adequate relief.

MIGRAINE HEADACHES

Migraine is one of the most common debilitating pain problems known, affecting about 17 percent of all women and roughly half as many men. The incidence and intensity of migraine is frequently increased around or during menstruation and often is associated with PMS. A significant number of female migraine victims abort their headaches by transdermal application of topical progesterone immediately at the onset of the headache, using up to 1 teaspoon of progesterone cream. In most women with migraine, it is worth trying this simple and often effective treatment.

Another natural adjunct in preventing migraine is the use of feverfew. But a word of caution: *Do not take feverfew during pregnancy, as it can lead to miscarriage.*

OVARIAN CYSTS AND MITTELSCHMERZ

Most women have an occasional ovarian cyst with some attendant pelvic pain. The failure of a follicle to ovulate lowers progesterone production for that cycle and creates an increased uterine congestion/proliferation or buildup of the uterine lining. With ovulation, an imbalance of FSH and LH leads to a corpus luteal cyst with temporary continuing progesterone production. Either situation, once diagnosed by pelvic exam, is likely to respond to the use of natural progesterone cream applied at approximately ½ teaspoon twice a day from the end of the period (approximately day 5) through day 26 or 28, continuing for several months. Decrease in size of the cyst may be monitored by pelvic exam or ultrasound.

Mittelschmerz, in a healthy woman, is a fairly normal and relatively minor painful occurrence at the time of ovulation. When a woman fails to ovulate, then the follicle may continue to swell with each month's cycle, increasing the size of, and possibly causing some bleeding into, the unovulated follicle. The cause is insufficient natural progesterone, which at normal levels would inhibit luteinizing hormone in a cyclical way. Contraceptive pills will aggravate the situation. The treatment of choice, therefore, is the addition of natural progesterone cream transdermally from the 10th or 12th day of the cycle up to the 26th to 28th day of the cycle, to suppress luteinizing hormone and shrink the follicle.

Even when cysts occur and become symptomatic, it is strongly advised that you try the regimen of natural progesterone cream in this cyclical fashion as described. If the size of the cyst does not decrease within two months, providing the necessary relief from pain, then other medical interventions may be indicated.

PELVIC INFLAMMATORY DISEASE

Pelvic inflammatory disease (PID) is a serious problem for many young women. Again, in a totally healthy vaginal state, the vagina is relatively resistant to infections. However, gonorrhea, chlamydia, and even the most common bacteria, *E. coli*, can cause an infectious process in the weakened vagina, uterus, and fallopian tubes. Pelvic inflammatory disease results when such an infection extends beyond the vagina, and is the most common cause of female infertility. Normal vaginal mucosa is often severely weakened by birth control pills and other synthetic hormones. Both contraceptive pills and synthetic progestins or Provera inhibit natural production of progesterone (and lower DHEA levels) and increase the risk of pelvic inflammatory disease, as does the number of sexual partners. One study, reported at the International Stress Congress in Montreux, has shown that women who have five or more sexual partners have an increased incidence of some type of pelvic infectious disease.

As with all problems that include weakness of the immune system, smoking also increases susceptibility to PID. Some women who regularly use hot tubs are susceptible to pelvic and bladder infections; pantyhose are also notoriously bad for pelvic health.

To avoid or minimize the possibility of this potentially serious illness:

1. Maintain a healthy lifestyle
   * Good nutrition: Minimize sugar, soft drinks, caffeine, and alcohol.
   * Exercise regularly, preferably for one hour, four to five days a week.
2. Avoid smoking
3. Avoid hot tubs
4. Avoid pantyhose
5. Maintain good menstrual health. If you have significant PMS, see the next section.
6. Minimize your number of sexual partners.

PMS

Premenstrual syndrome is a very common disorder among young women. Women who take birth control pills have a significant incidence of PMS. The symptoms generally occur seven to ten days prior to the menstrual cycle and include fatigue, headaches, loss of libido, irritation, depression, bloating, swelling, premenstrual weight gain, breast swelling or tenderness, and backache. Occasionally, PMS becomes so severe that it occurs three out of four weeks each month. Emotional stress and nutritional deficiencies, with a possible genetic predisposition, are obviously part of this syndrome. Generally, moderate doses of magnesium, vitamin B_6, and natural progesterone cream will satisfactorily control symptoms for the vast majority of patients with PMS. Stress reduction can be an important component of this.

Specific recommendations for PMS include:

- Use magnesium taurate, 375 mg daily, at bedtime. If improvement is not seen after the first month, increase dosage to 500 mg per day. Magnesium taurate is far better absorbed and better tolerated than any other form of magnesium. Remember that magnesium is a laxative. Magnesium taurate is available for sale at some health food stores.
- Use natural progesterone cream transdermally, ¼ teaspoon twice a day, days 10 through 28 of the cycle. If not improved after one month, go to ¼ teaspoon of natural progesterone cream four times daily, days 10 through 28.
- Do deep relaxation for fifteen minutes, twice a day.
- Exercise moderately at least five hours per week.
- Add chelated zinc, 30 mg per day.

TEMPOROMANDIBULAR JOINT (TMJ) SYNDROME

Over the last several decades, TMJ has become increasingly prevalent, particularly in menstruating women. Two epidemiological studies have demonstrated that oral contraceptives increase the incidence of TMJ. In addition, there is a 30 percent higher rate of TMJ syndrome in women who are receiving estrogen supplementation. Once again, part of TMJ therapy includes use of natural progesterone cream, ¼ teaspoon twice daily, days 10 or 12 to 26 to 28 of the cycle.

URINARY TRACT INFECTIONS

Some postmenopausal women have recurrent urinary tract infections, a condition that is much more serious than vaginitis, but, interestingly, is rare in women who use natural progesterone cream. In postmenopausal women, even one urinary tract infection should trigger the immediate use of intravaginal estriol cream, unless some other obvious problem such as yeast infections exists. I recommend use of natural progesterone cream along with the estriol cream. In four months, if all is going well, consider weaning from the estriol but continue the progesterone.

UTERINE FIBROIDS

Uterine fibroids are the most common form of tumors in the female urogenital tract. They are actually lumps of muscle and scar tissue that can grow to huge sizes. The largest one on record was over 100 pounds. Fibroids are often associated with very irregular bleeding (metrorrhagia) that can present as bleeding between periods, painful periods, dysmenorrhea or hypermenorrhea with excessive bleeding. Most often fibroids atrophy significantly after menopause. Too many women have unnecessary hysterectomies because of uterine fibroids. These tumors, like fibrocystic disease of the breasts, are the result of estrogen dominance created by anovulatory periods, as indicated earlier. When adequate natural progesterone is used, fibroid tumors cease growing and usually decrease in size.

Barring some clear-cut contraindication, the treatment of choice in all fibroids is natural progesterone cream. At the same time, it is essential that women with fibroids lose excess fat since fatty tissue produces estrogen, aggravating the imbalance. The vast majority of women with fibroids could avoid hysterectomy simply by losing excess weight and adding natural progesterone cream. From the viewpoint of health, safety, and cost, nothing can beat this remarkable alternative approach. Start with ¼ teaspoon twice a day, and if no improvement occurs within two to three months, increase to four times per day. If there is no improvement after four to six months, surgery may be required.

VAGINITIS

Inflammation or irritation of the vagina is common in pre-menopausal women, particularly in those who take birth control pills, or who have a dry vagina without lubrication prior to intercourse, possibly because of imbalance of progesterone and estrogen. Postmenopausally, vaginal dryness is also very common. The most successful treatment of post-menopausal dryness is the use of intravaginal estriol, which markedly decreases the incidence of urinary tract infection and improves lubrication, restoring the vagina back to "normal."

However, the transdermal use of natural progesterone cream alone will eventually relieve vaginal dryness and mucosal atrophy in a majority of women after three to four months of use. My personal recommendation for women who experience vaginal dryness is to use vitamin A and D ointment as a lubricant for three to four months, while waiting for the benefits of natural progesterone to kick in. If, after four months, the problem still persists, then continue progesterone and add intravaginal estriol as well. In either situation, vaginal mucosa and health will be markedly improved.

COMMONLY PRESCRIBED HORMONE REPLACEMENTS

PREMARIN

Premarin is the most common hormonal replacement used by women, with 22 million prescriptions written in 1996. Commonly called HRT or Hormonal Replacement Therapy, it should be called "Horse Replacement Therapy" since it is derived from the urine of mares.

I do not recommend Premarin because, in addition to a 43 percent increase of breast and/or uterine cancer, the following side effects have been noted:

Gallstones	Vaginal bleeding
Uterine fibroids	Bloating
High blood pressure	Water retention
Leg cramps	Headache
Lower DHEA	Nausea
Anxiety	Irritability

One of the main reasons that doctors prescribe Premarin is to guard against osteoporosis. Yet, studies show that this benefit disappears after five to ten years of use.

ESTRACE® AND ESTRADERM®

Unlike human estrogen, which is 60 to 80 percent estriol (the safest estrogen), 10 to 20 percent estradiol, and 10 to 20 percent estrone, Estrace and Estraderm are made up of only estradiol, the strongest form of estrogen. Estradiol is safest and best when used as part of triple estrogen just as Mother

Nature intended. The formula should include not more than 10 percent each estradiol and estrogen with 80 percent estriol. I recommend this triple estrogen for women who have had a complete hysterectomy.

PROVERA—ARTIFICIAL PROGESTERONE

Although the evidence is overwhelming that estrogen should be balanced with natural progesterone, most physicians prescribe synthetic Provera, which brings with it an increased risk of depression, weight gain, blood clots, cervical cancer, hair loss, and increased risk of heart disease, diabetes, and osteoporosis.[30,31]

Oral versus Transdermal Administration

There is only one known publication suggesting that transdermal progesterone is not effective.[32] There are many reporting the benefits, and even one that reports overdosing from topical progesterone cream.[33] In our clinic, blood levels of progesterone have been normalized appropriately with the use of natural progesterone cream. The increases in DHEA after topical progesterone also confirm its absorption.[34]

Oral administration of any hormone leads to a moderate loss of active hormone because before intestinal absorption the molecules are first carried through the liver, which begins chemical changes and decreases the "active" component. Despite this drawback, oral progesterone is widely used and significant blood levels are achieved. With oral administration, serum concentration is approximately three times as high when micronized progesterone in oil is used.

In general, transdermal application of progesterone and vaginal suppositories lead to blood levels similar to that achieved from micronized oral intake.

With estriol, it is known that transdermal or vaginal application allows it to bypass the liver, thus improving its overall blood level concentrations and the overall efficacy of estrogen.[35,36]

TESTOSTERONE

Throughout the life cycle, adrenal glands in men and women produce testosterone (although obviously in different amounts), which improves mood, muscle strength, bone strength, and libido. Testosterone supplementation is probably not needed if DHEA levels are optimal.

DHEA

DHEA (dehydroepiandrosterone) is perhaps even more crucial to health and longevity than is progesterone. The two together seem capable of providing the greatest advances to health maintenance seen in history. First, one must try to raise DHEA levels naturally. Many of the factors which optimize progesterone are equally beneficial in raising DHEA. These include sunlight (one-half to one hour daily); exercise; proper weight; avoiding smoking; and avoiding or minimizing intake of caffeine, soda, and sugar.

There is virtually no risk in proper supplementation of transdermal natural progesterone cream, which raises DHEA and provides all the other benefits of progesterone. Indeed, it may well be the DHEA enhancement of the progesterone that is responsible for at least some of the progesterone cream's beneficial effects. Both DHEA and progesterone:

• Are natural energizers/antidepressants
• Normalize blood sugar
• Help prevent obesity
• Optimize libido

DHEA is present in higher concentrations than any other hormone. Unfortunately, a majority of individuals begin to lose the ability to make adequate amounts of DHEA after age thirty, with most eighty-year-olds having blood levels only 10 percent of those of a healthy thirty-year-old.

However, some healthy eighty-year-olds have optimal DHEA levels with all its energy and health benefits. Even thirty-year-olds who are highly stressed may be deficient in DHEA.

DHEA significantly influences virtually all other hormones, including testosterone, estrogen, thyroid, and various pituitary hormones. As a single individual gauge of health, I recommend a blood test, but only through Quest Diagnostics or Meridian Valley Lab (see Resources). I have sent three to four blood samples from the same persons to six other different reference labs, disguising the clients' names, and found that all labs except Quest and Meridian gave values that varied on the same blood by 50 to 300 percent. That makes those other labs totally unreliable. Quest and Meridian are within 1 to 5 percent, which is very acceptable quality control.

For women at any age, if your level is 550 ng/dl or above, rejoice. For men, if your level is 750 ng/dl or above, celebrate. For women below 130 ng/dl or men below 180 ng/dl, I recommend supplementing with DHEA. For women, 25 to 75 mg per day and for men, 150 mg per day will be quite adequate. Those in between, that is, low but not deficient, should *not* take DHEA. Instead, they should use natural progesterone cream on the skin, ¼ teaspoon twice a day, and take Aqua-Power IV™, two per day. After six weeks, recheck DHEA levels. If approaching "good" levels (450 ng/dl in women and 600 ng/dl in men), continue. If not near these levels, obtain a prescription for one of the electrical stimulators found useful in raising DHEA when applied to twelve acupuncture points on the Ring of Fire.[37] (The Ring of Fire is an electrical circuit in the human body that energetically connects the kidneys, gonads, adrenals, thyroid, and pituitary glands.) I personally recommend primarily natural progesterone cream, ¼ teaspoon twice a day, for most postmenopausal women.

PREVENTING AND TREATING OSTEOPOROSIS

The single greatest cause of death in older women is complications from a fractured hip; it is all too common in men as well. Bone mass in women begins to decrease sometime after the mid-thirties. Although there has been some evidence that estrogen supplementation protects women from osteoporosis, the evidence is quite strong that it is effective only in the first three to five years of administration and has no significant protective effect after that. Furthermore, estrogen replacement without natural progesterone replacement leads to a marked increase in the incidence of cancer of the uterus and breast. Although Premarin decreases the incidence of heart disease in postmenopausal women, this protective effect is also lost after five to ten years, by which time frequency of incidence of breast cancer has begun to accelerate. That is why I advocate the use of natural progesterone.

Restoration of bone mass with estrogen alone is relatively ineffective. No study in which estrogen alone was supplemented has shown increase in bone mass. Note that the increasing loss of bone in women that begins in the mid-thirties occurs at the same time anovulatory periods begin and when progesterone levels are less than optimal. Estrogen enhances bone absorption and progesterone stimulates new bone formation.

Perhaps the most important factor in osteoporosis is inadequate calcium intake with estrogen dominance. Since a majority of adult Americans do not drink milk or eat adequate amounts of green leafy vegetables, calcium supplementation is essential. There is, however, considerable controversy over the bioavailability of milk calcium. Calcium absorption is decreased by a high–meat protein as well as a high-fat diet. Moreover, calcium cannot be incorporated into bone without adequate magnesium: 80 percent of American women and 70 percent of American men do not ingest even the recommended daily intake of magnesium. Calcium carbonate, which is the most common form of calcium in supplements, is the least well absorbed; calcium citrate is definitely better. Again, calcium citrate is significantly preferable for older women, because calcium absorption requires both adequate gastric acidity and vitamin D. Many elderly individuals do not make adequate hydrochloric acid to absorb calcium carbonate.

Phosphorus, the second most prevalent mineral in bone (which consists of a combination of calcium, phosphorus, and magnesium, in that order), is another component of the osteoporosis problem. Although phosphorus deficiency is virtually unknown, phosphorus excess is very common, primarily because of the very high intake of carbonated sodas that are loaded with phosphorus. Magnesium, the third most prevalent mineral in the bones and body, increases calcium absorption and facilitates its role in bone formation. Fertilizers used on crops grown for human and animal consumption often contain large amounts of potassium, which is a magnesium antagonist. In addition, sugar and alcohol increase urinary excretion of magnesium, as does stress. Most Americans should take 250 to 375 mg of magnesium taurate daily.

Zinc, manganese, boron, strontium, silicone, and copper are also essential in building bones, as are vitamins D, A, E, C, K, and B plus trace amounts of strontium and silicon.

Perhaps the most important habit to develop for building strong bones is adequate physical exercise including walking, jogging, using an exercise bicycle or a stair machine, or pursuing virtually any activity that gets the body moving and flexing on a regular basis without injury.

Factors that increase the risk of osteoporosis include obesity, excess intake of protein (especially red meats), diuretics (especially Lasix®), antibiotics which destroy the intestinal bacteria that make vitamin K, and fluoride, including that found in city water. Although fluoride increases the density of bone to some extent, it produces a more fragile bone. Alcohol intake, as indicated earlier, may cause magnesium loss and many other nutritional deficiencies.

OSTEOPOROSIS PREVENTION AND TREATMENT PROGRAM

1. Maintain optimal weight.
2. Exercise at least five hours per week, outdoors whenever possible. Sunlight in moderation is excellent for building DHEA and vitamin D.
3. Minimize or avoid sodas and sugar.
4. Take calcium citrate, 1,200 to 1,500 mg per day.
5. Take magnesium taurate, 375 mg per day.
6. Take daily:
   - 400 IU vitamin D
   - 3–5 mg boron
   - 25,000 IU beta carotene
   - 15–30 mg zinc gluconate or picolinate
   - 1 mg manganese
   - 3–5 mg copper (chelated)
   - 2,000 mg vitamin C
   - 25 mg vitamin B complex
   - 400–800 IU vitamin E
7. Regulate your menstrual periods with added natural progesterone cream on days 10 to 12 through days 26 to 28 of your cycle.
8. Postmenopausally, use ¼ teaspoon natural progesterone cream twice a day. If this does not control postmenopausal symptoms, add estriol.

9. Eat a low-fat diet with little red meat. Emphasize fish and chicken with lots of green, leafy vegetables and fruits.
10. If you have had a hysterectomy (with removal of ovaries), add estriol, 2.5 to 5 mg daily, transdermally if possible.[38, 39]

XENOESTROGENS AND THE ENVIRONMENT

Xenoestrogens, sometimes called organochlorides, are estrogenic compounds that encompass a wide variety of pesticides and other chemicals that have been introduced into our environment. Marked increase of these compounds in the last forty to fifty years is sometimes thought to be related to a variety of human illnesses, including increased breast and uterine cancer, and the increased incidence of male infertility. Although medical science is slow to pay attention to these influences, there is increasing evidence that this artificial, petrochemical, estrogenic increase in our environment is affecting animals by disrupting their ordinary mating procedures and markedly increasing the incidence of congenital malformations, especially in frogs.[40,41,42]

My first recommendation is to avoid all toxic pesticides and herbicides. Don't use them in your gardens or on your lawns. There are many safer alternatives, including corn gluten for weed control. For pest control, rotenone, pyrethrum, sabadilla dust, *bacillus thurgenesis*, and insecticidal soap can provide adequate and safe protection. Whenever possible, buy and eat organic foods to avoid xenoestrogens.

ALCOHOL AND ESTROGEN

Alcohol markedly increases estrogen levels in women who are taking Premarin as their hormonal replacement therapy. Drinking just a half glass of wine can increase estradiol by almost 100 percent, and if a woman drinks three glasses of wine, estradiol rises as much as 327 percent. This occurs within ten minutes after drinking alcohol, even before the maximum blood alcohol level is reached. Women who use any alcohol regularly, even one to two drinks per day, should be sure to exercise adequately and use natural progesterone at least days 12 to 28 of their cycle. Exercise is a proven stress reducer and regulator of metabolism. It is even more important than diet in maintaining health.

NATURAL PRECURSORS OF PROGESTERONE

There are many natural sources of the precursors of progesterone. The most striking is wild yam, but wild yam alone is not converted into progesterone in the body. It is reported that certain Polynesian women who consume large quantities of cooked wild yam remain fertile and free of common postmenopausal symptoms. Perhaps it is the quantity they consume. In a study done in my office, we found that 12 grams of dried wild yam root daily did not raise DHEA.

A wide variety of other vegetable products (currently estimated as close to five thousand) have been found to have the precursors to progesterone. Most common are soy, sarsaparilla, fennel, black and blue cohosh, dong quai, and many vegetables. Whether or not it is possible in our modern society to obtain nutritionally adequate progesterone precursors is probably a moot question for most of us. We simply can't eat enough precursors to be beneficial. Thus, natural progesterone cream in which the conversion has already been made is my recommendation of choice for both men and women. In women who have any of the signs of estrogen dominance, natural progesterone seems appropriate unless they have ovarian, breast, or uterine cancer. We now know that progesterone blocks conversion of testosterone to dihydrotestosterone, so it is *safe* even in men with prostate cancer. Men over age fifty may benefit both in their mood and their libido and in enhanced levels of DHEA when they apply natural progesterone cream transdermally.

One published article reported no increase in serum progesterone after ten days of transdermal Pro-Gest®.[43] This article fails to convince me for these reasons:

1. In our studies, almost all individuals respond to transdermal natural progesterone (we have used both Pro-Gest and Nugesterone™), with an increase in DHEA. It requires from six to twelve weeks to achieve these results. It is quite possible that the progesterone cream is being "used" first to replenish other hormonal pathways. This use of natural progesterone is so effective that I received a patent on the process.

2. My own serum level of progesterone is above the "upper limit" of normal as a result of my using natural progesterone cream. We are currently testing others who have been on transdermal progesterone for a period of at least three months.

3. Migraine headaches can often be aborted with transdermal progesterone.
4. Many women who use natural progesterone cream have been able to normalize their irregular periods.
5. Many women control PMS with transdermal progesterone cream.

It is extremely important that you use *natural progesterone* cream. There are a number of "wild yam" creams which do not contain progesterone. Read the label carefully. Do not buy it if it does not prominently read "progesterone USP." All products mentioned in the Resources section of this book contain 3 percent natural progesterone.

Each person has to judge for himself or herself how much is needed. From ¼ teaspoon once a day to perhaps even ½ teaspoon four times a day might be the range. Most people do well with ¼ teaspoon twice a day applied to the skin.

In men we recommend application primarily to the scrotum, which has very vascular skin with minimal subcutaneous fat. In women it may be placed anywhere on the skin including the breasts, abdomen, thighs, back, buttocks, and so on. It may be advisable to apply to different skin areas on some sort of rotating basis, as progesterone can be stored in fatty tissue, making it less available. On the other hand, no scientific study has found the use of the same general skin area to be less efficacious.

NATURAL PRECURSORS OF ESTROGEN

There are also many phytoestrogens, including soybeans and licorice. These weakly estrogenic botanicals appear to be safe and effective when progesterone alone is not adequate to prevent menopausal symptoms. In a study done by Dr. B. W. Gushleff of St. Louis Women's Center in Lake St. Louis, Missouri, 87 percent of 381 menopausal women reported a significant decrease in hot flashes, sweating, headache, vertigo, heart palpitations, nervousness, sleep disturbances, and depression using a specific phytoestrogenic complex, Pro-Estron™. Dr. Gushleff believes that this natural phytoestrogen may even be protective against xenobiotic estrogens such as pesticides and petrochemicals. This is the first scientific report of an effective alternative to Premarin.[44,45,46,47,48]

HORMONALLY DEPENDENT CANCER IN WOMEN

Breast, uterine, and ovarian cancer are hormonally triggered. Indeed, even men with breast cancer probably have a relative excess of estrogen. As emphasized throughout this book, estrogen excess is highly undesirable. The good news is that progesterone balances or opposes estrogen. Thus, theoretically, progesterone might be helpful in these three female hormonally dependent cancers. However, the research crucial to answer this question has not yet been done.

Breast cancer occurs predominantly in premenopausal women with normal or high estrogen and low progesterone levels. Postmenopausally, breast cancer is markedly more common in women who take estrogen (Premarin) supplementation.

Interestingly, the success of surgery in breast cancer is statistically higher when surgery is done in the last half of the menstrual cycle, when progesterone is naturally higher. If you do need surgery for breast cancer, it seems wise to insist it be done after midcycle.

Estrogen inhibitors, such as tamoxifen, also help prevent recurrence. It appears likely that natural progesterone would have a similar effect and not have the many toxic effects of tamoxifen,[49] including cataracts, retinopathy, hypercalcemia, uterine cancer, liver damage and failure, loss of platelets, anemia, severe white blood cell depletion, excess vaginal bleeding, and loss of libido.

A first successful pregnancy before age thirty significantly protects women from breast cancer. Miscarriages and abortions may increase the risk of breast cancer, as does the absence of any full-term pregnancy.

Women who have had hysterectomy and oophorectomy (removal of ovaries) have reduced risk of breast cancer unless they are given replacement estrogen without the protection of natural progesterone.

Finally, women with low progesterone levels have 5.4 times the risk of developing premenopausal breast cancer and a tenfold increase in risk of death from all cancers.

Interestingly, estriol, the safest of the estrogens, is the dominant estrogen during pregnancy. Women with breast cancer also produce about 45 percent less estriol than women without breast cancer. High estradiol and estrone coupled with low progesterone set the stage for breast cancer development.

The same hormonal situation is found in uterine cancer. Long-term synthetic estrogen (estradiol, estrone, or Premarin) administration increases the risk for uterine cancer fifteen times over that of women who do not take these supplements. It seems very likely that breast and uterine cancer would be significantly reduced if all women with low progesterone levels, preferably tested about age thirty-five, were supplemented with natural progesterone.

Ovarian cancer is also related to the estrogen-progesterone interplay, but there are insufficient studies to determine whether progesterone supplementation would help prevent this disease. Nevertheless, just as I recommend DHEA levels be determined for everyone by age forty, I also recommend blood progesterone levels be determined for all women by age forty, and earlier if they have major PMS symptoms. Alternatively, all women with symptoms of estrogen dominance and/or progesterone deficiency should begin natural progesterone supplementation during the second half of their cycles. Much could be gained with little risk.

Some women with estrogen dominance need very careful adjustment of the dosage of natural progesterone in order to regulate their cycles properly. Some need more, some less, than the usual ¼ teaspoon twice a day. They may also need to explore different timing strategies, starting as early as the day after the menstrual period, but in general, stopping not later than the day the next period begins.

WHICH PROGESTERONE CREAM?

The good news is that natural progesterone can be recommended with confidence to everyone; however, until further studies are done, I hesitate to recommend progesterone to women with breast, ovarian, or uterine cancer, even though it is likely that progesterone is safe since the estrogen balance achieved with progesterone is so remarkably useful in preventing these cancers. For all other men and women over fifty years of age, I recommend the use of natural progesterone cream, ¼ teaspoon twice a day.

Of considerable importance is the fact that transdermally applied natural progesterone does not raise cortisone, testosterone, or estrogen levels even though progesterone is considered a precursor of these hormones. There are no reports of excessive blood levels of any of these end point hormones when progesterone is administered.[50] Beyond any reasonable doubt, progesterone is the safest known hormonal supplement.

At this time, I know that these sources of progesterone cream are reliable: Pro-Gest, Nugesterone, Life Changes™, and Aqua Power IV. For prescriptions filled by a compounding pharmacy, see Resources. Unfortunately, there is no concrete evidence that many over-the-counter "wild yam creams" have progesterone in them.

NATURAL PROGESTERONE: A HORMONE FOR ALL SEASONS AND ALL PEOPLE

Natural progesterone is clearly the hormone of choice for postmenopausal women and for men. It can be taken orally, rectally, or vaginally, but none of these routes is superior to transdermal application. Indeed, unless it is micronized, oral progesterone is less satisfactory.

Natural progesterone is the only known hormone that can be taken without suppressing the body's own production of that hormone. Three percent natural progesterone cream is a safe and effective supplement. It is easily absorbed through the skin. It can be used to treat a wide variety of problems, including alcoholism, cervical dysplasia or erosion, endometrial carcinoma, endometriosis, fibrocystic breast disease, hypothyroidism, ovarian cysts, pelvic inflammatory disease, premenstrual syndrome, temporomandibular joint syndrome, urinary tract infections, uterine fibroids, vaginitis, depression, migraine, and low libido.

At this time, I recommend that men and most women over the age of fifty use transdermal natural progesterone cream. As stated earlier, men who do add progesterone should also take saw palmetto, 160 mg twice a day. Women with uterine, breast, or ovarian cancer probably should not use progesterone.

Women should avoid Premarin, and all synthetic estrogens except estriol or triple estrogen, as noted earlier. They should avoid Provera and all unnatural, artificial progestins.

RESOURCES

Blood Testing for DHEA or Progesterone

Quest Diagnostics
2320 Schuetz Road
St. Louis, MO 63146-3417
1-800-288-7293

Meridian Valley Labs
24030 132nd Avenue, S.E.
Kent, WA 98042
1-800-234-6825

Natural Progesterone Cream

Pro-Gest
Transitions for Health
Portland, OR 97205
1-800-888-6814

Aqua Power IV and Nugesterone
Self-Health Systems
5607 S. 222nd Road
Fair Grove, MO 65648
(417) 267-2900

Life Changes
MW Labs
2002 52nd Street Extension
Savannah, GA 31405
(912) 236-9430
(912) 236-9388 Fax

Compounding Pharmacies

Thayer's Colonial Pharmacy
1101 E. Colonial Drive
Orlando, FL 328031
1-800-848-4809

Pharmacy Specialists of Central Florida, Inc.
650 Maitland Avenue
Altamonte Springs, FL 32701
1-800-224-7711

Magnesium Taurate

Self-Health Systems
5607 S. 222nd Road
Fair Grove, MO 65648
(417) 267-2900

A Recommended Newsletter for Much More Information

The John R. Lee, M.D. *Medical Letter*
P.O. Box 84900
Phoenix, AZ 88071
1-800-528-0559

BIBLIOGRAPHY

The Bulletin, July 29, 1997, p. 16.

Chakmakjian, Zaven, and Nannepaga Y. Zachariah. "Bioavailability of Progesterone with Different Modes of Administration." *The Journal of Reproductive Medicine,* 32, no. 6 (June 1987): 443–48.

Chang, K., et al. "Influences of Percutaneous Administration of Estradiol and Progesterone on Human Breast Epithelial Cell Cycle in Vivo." *Fertility and Sterility,* 63, no. 4 (April 1995): 785–91.

Fredricsson, B. "Steroid Metabolism and Morphologic Features of the Human Testis." *Journal of Andrology,* 10, no. 1 (January-February 1989): 43–49.

Grodstein, Francine, et al. "Postmenopausal Hormone Therapy and Mortality." *Journal of Medicine,* 336, no. 25 (June 19, 1997): 1769–75.

Hammar, M. "In Vitro Conversion of Progesterone in the Human Testis at Different Ages, Pathophysiological Conditions, and During Treatment with Estrogens or Gonadotrophic Hormones." *Archives of Andrology,* 14, no. 23 (1985): 143–49.

Hargrove, Joel T. "Absorption of Oral Progesterone Is Influenced by Vehicle and Particle Size." *American Journal of Obstetrics and Gynecology,* 161, no. 4 (October 1989): 948–51.

Lee, John R. *Natural Progesterone.* Sebastopol, Calif.: BLL Publishing, 1993.

Lee, John R. "Osteoporosis Reversal, the Role of Progesterone." *International Clinical Nutrition Review,* 10, no. 3 (1990): 384–91.

LeResche, Linda, et al. "Use of Exogenous Hormones and Risk of Temporomandibular Disorder Pain." *Pain,* 69 (1997): 153–60.

Long, Cecil A. "Progesterone Concentration as a Predictor of Pregnancy Normalcy Is the Most Useful When HCG Levels Are Less than 2000 mIU/mL*." *Journal of Assisted Reproduction and Genetics,* 12, no. 3 (1995): 195–97.

MacLeod, S.C. "Endocrine Effects of Oral Contraception." *International Journal of Gynecology and Obstetrics,* 16, no. 6 (1978–79; 1995): 518–24.

McPherson K. "Oestrogens and Breast Cancer: Exogenous Hormones." *British Medical Bulletin,* 47, no. 2 (April 1991): 484–92.

Ottosson, U., et al. "Subfractions of High-Density Lipoprotein Cholesterol During Estrogen Replacement Therapy: A Comparison Between Progestogens and Natural Progesterone." *Journal of Obstetrics and Gynecology,* 151 (March 15, 1985): 746–50.

Prior, J.C. "Progesterone as a Bone-Trophic Hormone." *Endocrine Reviews,* 11, no. 2 (May 1990): 386–98.

Raloff, Janet. "The Gender Benders." *Science News,* 14 (January 8, 1994): 24–27.

Reyes, F., J. Winter, and C. Faiman. "Pituitary-Ovarian Relationships Preceding the Menopause." *American Journal of Obstetrics and Gynecology,* 129, no. 5 (November 1, 1977): 557–64.

Safe, S.H. "Environmental and Dietary Estrogens and Human Health: Is There a Problem?" *Environmental Health Perspectives,* 103, no. 4 (April 1995): 346–51.

Science News, January 8, 1994, pp. 24–27.

Stevenson, J., et al. "Effects of Transdermal versus Oral Hormone Replacement Therapy on Bone Density in Spine and Proximal Femur in Postmenopausal Women." *The Lancet,* 336 (August 4, 1990): 265–69.

Tesarik, J. "Selective Expression of a Progesterone Receptor on the Human Sperm Surface." *Fertility and Sterility,* 58, no. 4 (October 1992): 784–92.

Weiss, Rick. "Estrogen in the Environment." *The Washington Post,* January 25, 1994.

Wright, Jonathan V., et al. *Natural Hormone Replacement.* Petaluma, Calif.: Smart Publications, 1997.

REFERENCES

1. F. Grodstein et al. 1997. "Postmenopausal Hormone Therapy and Mortality," *The New England Journal of Medicine* 336 (25): 1769–75.
2. C. N. Shealy et al. 1995. "Electrical Stimulation Raises DHEA and Improves Diabetic Neuropathy," *Stress Medicine* 11: 215–17.
3. *History of Progesterone as Described by Goodman and Gilman, The Pharmacological Basis of Therapeutics,* 6th ed. 1980, 1420.
4. "Molecular Transformation of Plant Sources to Progesterone," *Cancer Forum* 13 (5/6), Winter 1994–95.
5. *History of Progesterone,* 1420.
6. U. B. Ottosson, B. G. Johansson, and B. von Schoultz. 1985. "Subfractions of High-Density Lipoprotein Cholesterol During Estrogen Replacement Therapy: A Comparison Between Progestogens and Natural Progesterone," *American Journal of Obstetrics and Gynecology* 151 (6): 746–50.
7. *History of Progesterone,* 1420.
8. *History of Progesterone,* 1420.
9. J. R. Lee, *Natural Progesterone: The Multiple Roles of a Remarkable Hormone* (Sebastopol, Calif.: BLL Publishing, 1993).
10. *History of Progesterone,* 1420.
11. Lee, *Natural Progesterone.*
12. R. A. Edgren. "Progestins," *Clinical Use of Sex Steroids* (Yearbook Medical Publishers, Inc., 1980).
13. Lee, *Natural Progesterone.*
14. *History of Progesterone,* 1420.
15. F. I. Reyes, J. S. D. Winter, and C. Faiman. 1977. "Pituitary-Ovarian Relationships Preceding the Menopause," *American Journal of Obstetrics and Gynecology* 129: 557–64.
16. Lee, *Natural Progesterone.*
17. Ibid.

18. Ibid.
19. Ibid.
20. S. H. Safe. 1995. "Environmental and Dietary Estrogens and Human Health: Is There a Problem?," *Environmental Health Perspectives* 103 (4): 346–51.
21. C. P. Barsano and J. A. Thomas. 1992. "Endocrine Disorders of Occupational and Environmental Origin," *Occupational Medicine* 7 (3): 479–502.
22. S. C. MacLeod. 1978–79. "Endocrine Effects of Oral Contraception," *International Journal of Gynecology and Obstetrics* 16 (6): 518–24.
23. J. Veldscholte et al. 1990. "Unusual Specificity of the Androgen Receptor in the Human Prostate Tumor Cell Line LNCaP: High Affinity for Progestagenic and Estrogenic Steroids," *Biochimica Et Biophysica Acta* 1052 (1): 187–94.
24. J. Tesarik et al. 1992. "Selective Expression of a Progesterone Receptor on the Human Sperm Surface," *Fertility and Sterility* 58 (4): 784–92.
25. B. Fredricsson, K. Carlstrom, and L. Ploen. 1989. "Steroid Metabolism and Morphologic Features of the Human Testis," *Journal of Andrology* 10 (1): 43–49.
26. Lee, *Natural Progesterone.*
27. J. V. Wright and J. Morgenthaler, *Natural Hormone Replacement* (Petaluma, Calif.: Smart Publications, 1997).
28. J. R. Lee. 1990. "Osteoporosis Reversal, The Role of Progesterone," *International Clinical Nutrition Review* 10 (3): 384–91.
29. Lee, *Natural Progesterone.*
30. Grodstein et al. "Postmenopausal Hormone Therapy," 1769–75.
31. Lee, *Natural Progesterone.*
32. A. Cooper et al. 1998. "Systemic Absorption of Progesterone from Progest Cream in Postmenopausal Women," *The Lancet* 351 (9111): 1255–56.
33. E. F. Ilyia, D. McLure, and M. Y. Farhat. 1998. "Topical Progesterone Cream Application and Overdosing," *The Journal of Alternative and Complementary Medicine* 4 (1): 5–6.
34. Shealy, "Electrical Stimulation Raises DHEA," 215–17.
35. Lee, *Natural Progesterone.*
36. Z. H. Chakmakjian and N. Y. Zachariah. 1987. "Bioavailability of Progesterone with Different Modes of Administration," *The Journal of Reproductive Medicine* 32 (6): 443–48.
37. Shealy, "Electrical Stimulation Raises DHEA," 215–17.
38. Lee, *Natural Progesterone.*
39. Lee, "Osteoporosis Reversal," 384–91.

40. Safe, "Environmental and Dietary Estrogens," 346–51.
41. Barsano, "Endocrine Disorders," 479–502.
42. J. Raloff. 1994. "Are Environmental 'Hormones' Emasculating Wildlife?" *Science News* 14: 24–27.
43. A. Cooper et al. 1998. "Systemic Absorption of Progesterone from Progest Cream in Postmenopausal Women," *The Lancet* 351 (9111): 1255–56.
44. H. Aldercreutz. 1990. "Diet, Breast Cancer, and Sex Hormone Metabolism," *Annals New York Academy of Sciences* 595: 281–90.
45. P. L. Horn-Ross. 1995. "Phytoestrogens, Body Composition, and Breast Cancer," *Cancer Causes and Control* 6: 567–73.
46. H. Aldecreutz et al. 1986. "Determination of Urinary Ligans and Phytoestrogen Metabolites, Potential Antiestrogens and Anticarcinogens in Urine of Women on Various Habitual Diets," *Journal of Steroid Biochemistry* 25: 791–97.
47. G. Wilcox et al. 1990. "Oestrogenic Effects of Plant Foods in Postmenopausal Women," *British Journal of Medicine* 301: 905–06.
48. B. W. Gushleff. 1998. "Pro-Estron™: A Technical and Practical Guide for the Physician and Patient," *Longevity News Network*.
49. *Physician's Desk Reference*, 52d ed. (Montvale, N.J.: Medical Economics Company, 1998).
50. Lee, *Natural Progesterone*.